# *Slipstream* Stories

## Return to the Source

by Sonny Spots

I LOVE INDIA

www.slipstreamstories.com

ISBN: 978-0-6151-4786-4

# *Stories:*

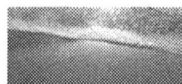

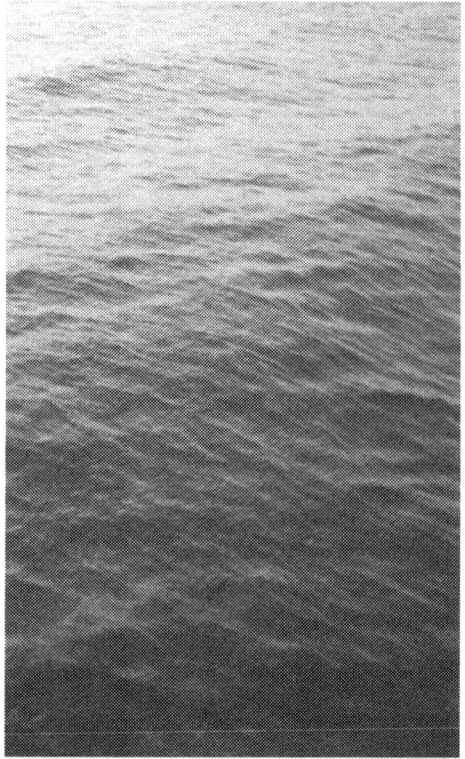

SLIPSTREAM STORIES

Before "Gigli," I worked on the star-studded (George Clooney, Brad Pitt, Julia Roberts, Matt Damon, Andy Garcia, Bernie Mac, Elliot Gould, Eddie Jemison, Casey Affleck, Scott Caan, Don Cheadle, Carl Reiner, Shaobo Qin), Steven Soderbergh directed, "Ocean's 11" and with the good pay and extra on-the-road compensation I was able to buy a new car. Actually, the Saab hatchback was previously driven but new to me and in new condition.

I selected it based on a few quali-fications. For one, it needed to be fast so that I could get in and out of LA for the weekend at record speeds. Two, it needed to be comfortable for the daily commut-ing, including air conditioning and a good stereo. And three, I should be able to easily slide a fly-fishing rod into it without having to break it down for my expeditions into the Sierra Nevada Mountains.

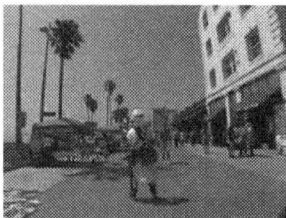

The Saab qualified on all counts and the stereo exceeded my expectations with amazing sound. The six-CD changer paired with Hear Music, a music store on the Third Street Promenade in Santa Monica, led me to find myself…musically. With a high quality selection and listening stations, I could always find just the right tune. So, I rode back and forth to that office, listening.

Eventually, the shooting of the movie wrapped, the days grew longer and my hours at the office became shorter. I began to discover the life of the street I lived on. I started taking in the evenings and weekends on the front porch of my apartment with my friend John, a fifty-something year old writer whom I met while working on a movie in Sante Fe, New Mexico.

Horizon Avenue received a constant breeze, a gift from the Pacific Ocean, and John called it, "The street of pretty girls." Jenni, a transplanted New York massage therapist with hair the same color as her golden Labrador Retriever, Harley, was the first to be "Sucked into our bullshit," as John would put it and soon we had half the block sitting on the porch with us.

It was one of those Horizon Avenue porch evenings that awaited me on the night of the accident. I had been doing some clean-up work on the movie "XXX." I spent a long week and a day in a Burbank office building adjacent to Warner Bros. and Universal Studios sorting through a mess of documents and preparing reports for a possible insurance company audit of a claim made due to the director's back injury.

I was thrilled when I was finally released. I emerged from the underground parking and within minutes was rolling into the sunset on the 101 North listening to a CD called Genetic World by Telepopmusik, the track was called Breathe, with the predominant lyric, "Another day".

The traffic was moving along smoothly until, suddenly, the car ahead of me, a grey Chevy Lumina, came to an abrupt halt. I in turn did the same, but behind me from the parallel lane, a blue Chevy pick-up truck came crashing into the rear of my Saab, jolting me forward and spinning the car a bit sideways into the Lumina.

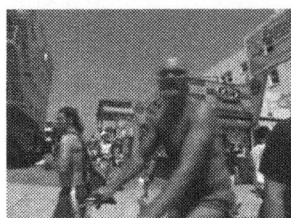

The impact felt like a mallet over the xylophone of my spinal cord and after getting the battered vehicles to the side of the freeway and giving our reports to the California Highway Patrol men and woman, I was strapped onto a hard wooden board and transported to the nearest hospital.

In the emergency room, I lay strapped to the board facing the ceiling for quite a while until a doctor who appeared to be overworked like an only waitress in an all-night diner finally saw me and sent me for x-rays. She didn't see anything in the x-rays to be concerned about, so I was un-strapped and sent away with a couple of prescriptions for pain relief and reduction of inflammation.

I took a taxi to the wrecking yard to get my CD's from the changer under the crumpled-in hatchback. I had to fold down the back seats to reach them but the retrieval was a success. The attendant at the yard pointed out a crinkle in the frame above the passenger side door and said it should be the determining factor that the car would be declared a total loss.

The next morning, I woke up sore, stiff, and with a serious headache. I also received a phone call from a radiologist, who told the doctor I went to see that afternoon, that he noticed a "crinkle" in the x-ray. The solemn doctor prescribed physical therapy and more pills.

I began the physical therapy at the clinic provided by my health plan where I saw the doctor. But after a few visits of electro-stimulation and hot packs I felt like I needed something more proactive and something closer to where I lived.

Beyond Physical Therapy was an easy bicycle ride from Horizon and the Pilates based program was just what I needed. Pilates is a technique centered on the idea of strengthening your inner core, your deep abdominals, attained by practicing various exercises.

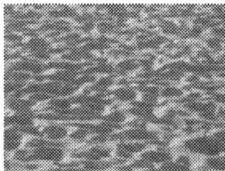

After Beyond, I moved to the Soma Syntax Studio. I wanted to continue with Pilates and Anne Sotelo also utilized Rolfing, a hands-on technique to put the body in its place. We would talk of all kinds of things, from dogs to the Dalai Lama.

The magic pocket of Venice and Santa Monica also offered three fantastic farmer's markets, all within a walk or bicycle ride. I began to feel better and my exercise program increased to runs along the beach and even some minor gymnastics on the equipment at the old "Muscle Beach" beneath the Santa Monica Pier. I also began practicing yoga at one of the many studios in the area.

With all of the therapy, exercise, and nutrition I felt like the bionic man...being rebuilt...stronger, faster, smarter and there was more. I began to sense something new about myself, but something that felt like it had always been there. It was like a connection to a greater sense of being, a force that engulfed me.

I first identified it on one of my evening walks along the Venice Boardwalk while listening to music from the ipod mp3 player I received as a crew gift from Jennifer Lopez and Ben Affleck and then found it more and more, day by day. I called it the *slipstream* and it changed the course of my life.

# Suitcase

You could say I was sidewalk surfing when I felt my mobile phone vibrate in my pocket.

"Hello," I answered.

"Hey bro, what's up? Where are you at right now?" asked my brother Jake.

"I'm in Venice, skateboarding out on the board-walk."

"Isn't it a little late there?" he asked.

"Yeah, it's great, lots of room to carve out some turns."

He asked me to fly to Singapore to meet him where we would collect his boat that had been shipped atop a freighter from the States and captain it up the pirate infested Malacca Straits to a marina in Phuket, Thailand.

"I'm in," I answered.

Jake had a panicked look on his face when I met him at the baggage claim.

"Let's go, quick," he said.

In the taxi, he told me he had some crazy Thai woman following him. Well, not just any woman but someone he had been dating, and he ditched her at the airport.

She had a friend that worked for the airline and somehow unexpectedly ended up in the seat behind him on his flight to Singapore, tapping him on his shoulder, "Hi Jake."

We stayed at a different hotel than where he had made the reservation to avoid being found. When we were ready to go, Jake called the bell desk to pick up our bags we left outside the door of our room and we went to check out. A bellman loaded the bags into the taxi and we were driven to the Port of Singapore Authority Pass Office.

We unloaded our bags out onto the street, six of them in all, a black leather rucksack with a matching garment bag, a black duffel bag, a tan garment bag, a black leather brief-case and a large black rectangular nylon roller bag. We had moved two of the bags from the street to the office when "The Doctor" arrived. We were told that this was the name given to him by his co-workers, due to his knack for problem solving and putting the right operation into action.

"Yankee", a thirty-eight foot sport-fishing boat, sat on a cradle at the edge of the dock beneath the massive cranes steadily loading and unloading containers onto and off of the cargo ships. Jake and I loaded the bags into Yankee and then climbed down a ladder and jumped onto the deck of a tugboat in the harbor. A team of men strapped belts underneath the belly of the boat. One of the massive cranes rolled over, hoisted the boat, dropped her in the water, and off we went with a blow of the horn and a wave of thanks to the Doctor.

Checking the instruments, Jake found that the only thing working was the radar. The GPS satellite-mapping system required a chip for the area that we didn't have, the depth finder wasn't operational and neither was the radio.

Our first stop was Raffles Marina at the top of the island across from Malaysia where Johnny Lim would help us stack the tower which provided a higher view to pilot from, had sleeves for fishing rods and supported the outriggers.

We spent the remainder of the day preparing the boat. The Doctor drove all the way across the island to give us some immigration documents and two blue baseball caps with an eagle stitched in red above the bill. We gleamed at how everything had run like clockwork.

In the evening, we went to the bar to eat. The kitchen was already closed so we settled for pretzels and large, giant, steins of beer.

"Welcome," sang the two Filipino girls dancing on the stage, a third played the keyboard and ran the background music.

At the break, Jake bought the girls some drinks and they came over and sat with us. Jake spent some time in the Philippines and when they asked where he had been and he replied, "Mandaluyong," they asked "Inside or out?" referring to the insane asylum there. They were so fun and lively that Jake nicknamed them, "The Spunksters."

We slept in the cabin of the boat that night and woke early with hopes of setting off up the Straits. A guy from the marina hollered to us, "Immigration in fifteen minutes," but nobody showed up to stamp us out of Singapore so we left to go shopping for provisions and attempted to source the GPS chip we needed and good color charts of the area.

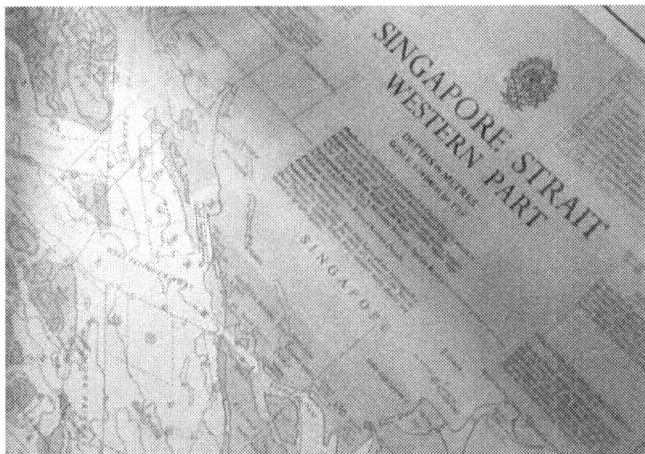

We didn't find either. All we had were black and white photocopies of charts given to Jake by his friend, Khun Jim in Thailand, to navigate our way up the Straits. When we returned, we found we had missed the immigrations officer so they had to call him back. We went for another night of "The Spunksters" and Jake told them we stayed just to see them again. They were all smiles and said they were flattered.

We set off at the dawn's early light, but we were bound to hit a few foul balls and eventually strike out in Lankawi, Malaysia.

First, we missed the Malacca Straits and ended up at the coast of Indonesia asking a couple of local fishermen, "Which way to Port Dixon?"

All we got were big smiles, waves and nods.

"Can you just show us on the map where we are?" we pleaded.

Next, we sucked a big rope onto the prop, seizing up the engines. These were just the foul balls.

Just after we were congratulating ourselves, "We can do this!"

Penang is where the curve balls started coming. Expecting a grand Penang Yacht Club, which had gone out of business, we passed up our only chance of a marina with fuel due to its rickety graveyard appearance and its incomprehensible fueling system.

Strike one came in when we were attempting to ask some local guys out of a shed on the dock of a fish farm, "Yacht club, marina, fuel?"

Boom, fastball! We sucked up a net along with meters of rope attached to a jug that covered the prop and ran up the shaft. Jake spent hours in the water cutting it up along with his hands and after he unsuccessfully attempted to swim to shore for a cigarette we spent the night anchored out eating Tom Yum flavored Cup-O-Noodles.

Strike two, a missed bunt, hit us when we ran out of fuel just as we were pushing off from Omar's dock who at first couldn't give us any fuel but then orchestrated our return to sea, including bleeding the engine, providing a driver to an ATM for Malaysian Ringa and 7 Eleven for cigarettes and getting us fuel from the police fuel dock. He liked us to call him "Omar Shariff" and we considered him our Penang hero.

Strike three was a drop ball as the bearing dropped out the prop just as we were backing into a slip at the Royal Lankawi Yacht Club. Feeling lucky that it happened there, we decided to cut our losses. Strike three we were out. Jake hired the dock supervisor, Raden, who oversaw the boat's repair that required it to be hoisted back out of the water, to safely deliver the boat to Phuket.

We packed up our bags, wheeled them off the dock on a dolly and took a cab over to a beautiful resort hotel we had passed on our way in. We went to the room, unloaded our bags, shared a beer on the balcony and went for a dip in the pool. It was so refreshing and relieving to know we would be sleeping in nice beds on land. Even the wobbling feeling that I was rocking back and forth, side to side began to ease.

After observing the boat repair at the dry dock across the bay, we rode in the yacht club van back to town and Jake got Raden set with fuel money for the boat. They dropped us off at the hotel and we packed our bags and took a taxi to the ferry terminal. It was packed with people and bags but we got on and got moving over the water.

We arrived in southern Thailand and took a taxi to Hat Yai where we spent the night and I ate one of the most "pit" (meaning spicy hot in Thai) meals I have ever tasted. The Three Crispy Salad was a mixture of Thai chilies.

The next morning we had breakfast at the hotel and took a taxi to the Hat Yai airport where we caught the twenty-five U.S. dollar flight to Phuket. We had to pay an extra five dollars for overweight bags. The flight was a quick up and down at about an hour. Wow, did it feel great to get to Phuket.

Our first business was to gather our dirty clothes to take to the laundry service. I took my bags up to the guest room and began to unload them. Jake brought up the large roller bag we had been traveling with and set it by the door to my room. I carried it over to his room.

"What?  Do you just want to store this bag in my room?" he asked.

"What do you mean? This is your bag," I replied.

"No, it isn't," he answered.

We deduced that the bag must have been loaded into the taxi at the hotel in Singapore and all along we both thought it to be the others. We had lugged that bag around Singapore, into the boat, up the Malacca Straits, around Lankawi and onto the packed ferry, every taxi we rode in we had to put bags up on the passenger seat, and we even paid the excess baggage fee to bring it on the flight from Hat Yai.  Now what do we do with it?

We inspected the bag to find it locked with no nametag. In the pocket on the back was a medical x-ray with a woman's name on it but no contact information.  Our time in Phuket was brief and Jake knew there was a hotel of the same chain in Delhi, India where we would be flying to next.  So the bag from Singapore went with us to India but at a premium, another excess baggage fee of fifty dollars.

He took the bag to the hotel and explained the situation to the front desk. They said that the hotels were franchises and they would not accept it. Jake made a run for it.  He left the bag, jumped into his car and told his driver, "Let's go!"  But before Jake could make his getaway, the hotel staff lowered the gate, brought the bag to the car and hastily threw it into the trunk.

The next day, Jake received a call from the hotel in Singapore saying that someone was missing the bag and they really needed to get it back. Jake suggested that as he already attempted to return it, they should send someone to pick it up. The man he spoke with said this was difficult for him, as he didn't have the resources in Delhi.

"Would you please just drop it off at the hotel in Delhi," he pleaded.

The next day, Jake's driver dropped the bag at the hotel.

Quite some time had passed and at a company celebration Jake met a guy, "The Doc," but an Indian Doc and not the Doctor from Singapore, who was a guest of honor at the celebration. He was a vintage car enthusiast and invited Jake and my mother to join them to ride in a Lancaster straight-eight at the head of a parade in Mysore, India. "Why not," they thought, "It should be a real India experience."

In Mysore, there was a lot of shuffling and moving bags in and out of the vintage cars and Jake told the Doc and the group our bag story. They all got a really good laugh out of it.

Back in Delhi, the Doc was visiting and told Jake there was someone he wanted him to meet. It was the general manager of the hotel in Delhi. He went to his house in the outskirts of town where he had a collection of classic American cars and a completely restored bogey from the Palace on Wheels, a train car previously used to tour India by a maharaja.

The general manager told Jake that the suitcase had been the talk of the hotel. The woman who lost it, had attorneys file a lawsuit against the hotel in Singapore for loosing her bag which she claimed was full of valuables. Once it was returned to the hotel in Delhi it sat for months, still locked, waiting for her attorneys along with the attorneys representing the hotel to open it together and inspect its contents.

The people at the hotel in Delhi were all very curious, "What could be in that bag?"

When they opened it, all they found were clothes and at the time the general manager told the story to Jake, he suspected that the case was still in litigation.

# Highest Road

With a flashlight in hand to light the way, I walked along Changspa Lane to the center of Leh situated at an altitude of 3505 meters with the world's highest airport set amidst the stark mountains of Ladakh, India's northernmost region bordered by Pakistan and what is now the Tibetan region of China. It's a land filled with many of the world's "highest's" and on that morning, I was on my way to catch a bus over the world's highest motorable pass.

I was early for the five-thirty a.m. scheduled departure and the bus didn't show up until seven. Mostly locals and a few foreign travelers filled the seats and on the way out of town we stopped for more passengers who camped in the aisle.

Riding a bus in Ladakh is like attending a rolling party. The driver cum DJ pops the cassette tapes into a player mounted onto the dash decorated with flashing lights and the Ladakhi's pass around treats of snacks and candies.

We chugged uphill out of Leh, whipping around hair-raising switchback turns, until the bus stopped at a checkpoint. People got off the bus to answer the call of nature and buy snacks from tented shops.

After an authority inspected our papers, we ascended into a white mist of snow. The man seated next to me pointed out strings of colorful prayer flags and said, "Highest gompa in the world." Gompa means monastery.

Soon, I saw people posing next to the sign, "Khardung La, World's Highest Motorable Pass 5602 meters." Our bus kept on rolling over the summit and descended along the road carved into the steep mountainside until it stopped behind a string of vehicles.

We waited for the fragile road to be repaired by the always-employed crew and then passed over the rollercoaster of bumps that lifted me from my seat. The bus continued along the winding road to smoother conditions below. Riding along the edge of a steep river canyon, I could see isolated villages dotting the terraced mountainsides in the distance.

After another passport check, we reached Khalsar where we stopped and spread out among the restaurants and tea stands. I sat outside, slurped up noodles from a bowl of vegetable thukpa soup and sipped a chai (milk tea). A rainbow of multi-colored trucks lined the road waiting for their turn to cross over the pass.

The bus dropped down into the expanding Nubra Valley and when we reached Sumur I got off. As the bus disappeared in the distance, I took a look around the vast sparsely inhabited landscape. "What am I doing here?" I thought. A man who had also gotten off the bus pointed me in the direction of a guesthouse.

After a short walk, I entered through a steel gate. I negotiated a room, placed my dinner order for mo mos and set off to explore the area. The man seated next to me on the bus had told me of a nearby gompa I could visit that the Dalai Lama had recently stayed at in a house the monks had built specifically for that purpose.

It was a lovely walk along a small babbling stream lined with bright yellow seabuckthorn berry bushes.

I discovered a stupa with colorful haloed Buddhas painted on a cracked cement wall and soon came upon my friend from the bus.

He walked me up to the gompa and left me at its' entrance.

It was brilliantly painted white with red and gold. Inside, several of the doorways were surrounded with intricate vibrant patterns. I found a nice spot and sat absorbing the sounds of the nearby stream.

When I left, I waved to a group of young novice monks and crossed a bridge where two children came running down to greet me.

"One photo," they cried.

The young girl and boy were very friendly and I noticed the novice monks watching as I took photos of them. The girl took my hand and led me up to her family's enclave of small rooms set around a courtyard.

They invited me in for tea and biscuits. The family was from Nepal, they told me as we sipped butter salt tea. The young girl sat beside me with her hand on my arm. We joked and laughed and took some more photos and then they made a rice wine called chang from powdered balls they purchased at the market in Diskit, the nearest town. Not bad, but not for me.

It was nearing dusk and one of the guys suggested I begin my walk back to the guesthouse before night fell. Along a small road through the village, I came upon a prayer wheel with "Om Mani Padme Hum" painted in Tibetan text. "Om Mani Padme Hum" has many meanings and is said not to be accurately translatable to English but a rough literal translation is, "The jewel of the lotus of the heart," and as a mantra, "Om Mani Padme Hum," is said to purify and evoke compassion on the path to enlightenment.

I gave it a spin and continued walking. I listened to the ringing of the attached bell fade as the distance grew.

"Julley" said a group of Ladakhi's I passed and "Julley" I replied.

If you should know one word in Ladakhi, it's "Julley" meaning "Hello, goodbye" or "How are you?" "I'm fine" and "Thank you, your welcome" depending upon the inflection and situational context. The most popular song in Ladakh is the happy sounding Julley song. It's like the national anthem and the lyric, "Julley."

At the guesthouse, I sat beneath the canopy of a parachute with a French man wearing something like a smoking jacket enjoying a cigar. We were joined for a delicious dinner of mo mos (circles of dough wrapped around a filling of vegetables) and boiled baby potatoes by another man and woman who were also from France. The woman was the life of the party with her smiling eyes and lively conversation. She insisted to speak in English as to include me.

I woke up early the next morning and feeling quite satisfied with my visit, decided to try to catch the bus back over the pass, as it was the journey over the highest road that intrigued me most.

I found everyone waiting at the roadside and was lucky to get a seat when the bus finally showed up. The transmission broke down about three times making it questionable whether we would make it to the peak or not.

It reminded me of a story called, The Little Engine That Could, "I think I can, I think I can, I think I can... I know I can," and over the pass we went.

# Bambu House

I was stringing a mosquito net over the bed in the "Bambu House" when I heard a hello from outside. I stepped out to the front door to find a young couple standing there.

"We really like your house and wonder how long you'll be staying in it?" the guy said.

"I just moved in this morning and I plan to stay awhile," I replied.

The girl looked surprised. She asked what time I had moved in that day. She started explaining that she had asked for a room around the same time, but before she finished her story, her boyfriend interrupted her. He looked at me, "Well, lucky you."

I watched them walk away and wondered if it was really luck.

Nearly two weeks before, as I looked for my name on the dot matrix boarding manifest taped outside the red and yellow train car, a man standing on the platform urged me to get in. I boarded the Trivandrum Rajdhani Express just as it was pulling away from the H. Nizamuddin Railway Station in Delhi.

I stepped aboard and walked the aisle to find a man in my assigned seat. I accommodated his request to switch so that he and his wife could be together for what the Indian Railways called the "Happy Journey." It was a smooth and comfortable overnight ride to the Madgaon Station in Goa where I disembarked. I had come to Goa to explore the area with hopes of finding a good place to do some writing.

Standing on the platform, waiting for the local train to Palolem, I said hello to a long, brown-haired roundish woman standing beside me who had a friendly smile.

"Where are you going?" I asked.

"Gokarna, and you?"

"Palolem," I replied.

"Oh, I'm actually going to meet a friend in Gokarna who just left Palolem, she didn't like it, she was pissed at all the loud music," she said.

But my report was different. I had received an e-mail from a couple of girls from California I had met in Varanasi that described the long beaches lined with palm trees and the warm water.

After I spent over a week in Palolem, I would have to agree with both reports. I loved it. But I didn't accomplish much writing. The beautiful sites and all-night music kept me distracted. However, I was patient, I thought that in my travels when the time was right I would find the ideal place.

I decided to head off for Gokarna in the state of Karnataka just to the south of Goa. The woman I had spoken with at the Madgaon Station had recommended Gokarna.

I stepped off the platform into a crowded car, benches of three blue seats across from more benches of blue seats full of Indian men in simple collared shirts and slacks and Indian women, some dressed in colorful saris and some with flowers in their hair.

Instead of rushing around to find a seat, I was happy to stand near the doorway, next to a few comic Indian men, who using their hands, motioned that another had been drinking. They spilled a chai, all over the floor. A few minutes down the tracks I stopped a newly boarded man from setting his bag on the light brown translucent chai covered floor.

At a stop about halfway through the trip, a few people got off the train and another Indian man showed me a vacant seat and asked me to sit down. Hot but comfortable wind rushed in from the barred windows as we zipped past landscapes of backwater marshes, coconut trees, and occasional green rolling hills.

When we arrived at the Gokarn Road Railway Station I slipped off the train behind a couple of other backpackers. From the platform, I could see a mob of travelers below.

I stepped back and took a bottle of water from the snack bar. I asked the boy who worked there about getting into town.

"You can take the Ashram bus parked below to Gokarna for 20 rupees," he answered.

I went down and was lucky to get a seat. I found that many of these travelers were part of one large group standing around negotiating their next move. On the bus ride, I spoke with some Australian girls to my left who were on an "around-the-world-in-seven-months-trip" as they put it with a sense of urgency in their voices and a young German guy, Patrick, to my right. He had only been in India a few days.

"My family is worried about me, I am traveling alone. I think it's a problem," he said.

"I don't think it's such a problem, traveling alone gives you great freedom," I replied.

When the bus stopped in Gokarna, I waited for Patrick to get his backpack and walked with him into town. At a crossroad lined with vendors selling everything from decorative textiles of every color imaginable and Hindu religious paraphernalia to children's toys, a couple joined us, also from Germany, and we all headed off toward the beach.

Walking beside several huge towering wooden chariots with wheels that dwarfed a person to half their size, we were reminded that this is one of the Hindu's holiest places.

When we got to the next crossroad just before Gokarna Beach, everyone pulled out their guidebooks.

"I read that Kudle Beach is just south of Gokarna," I said, pointing to the road that seemed the obvious choice.

As we began our descent to the beach, we noticed other backpackers ahead of us. I slowed down to give them space knowing that otherwise we would reach the beach at the same time and have to compete to get a room.

When we reached the "Looksea Guesthouse," the couple rushed in. They took the first little cave with a raised wood bed and a mattress pad. A boy showed us two more rooms, one had a sleeping pad and the other, a thatch hut, did not.

Although the room with the pad seemed all right for me, I decided to leave the choice to Patrick, as not to force him into the thatch hut or to continue searching. Patrick didn't seem to find the place to his liking so we continued our search.

The next spot I found more ideal. They had two small clay huts but only one had a sleeping pad. I felt OK with roughing it some but thought I wouldn't sleep well on a clay floor without a sleeping pad so I gave Patrick the option.

"You take the hut with the pad and I will continue the search or I will take the hut with the pad and you continue the search," I said. Patrick opted to take the hut.

I continued on to find the next place the same, no pad, and the one after that was full. I ran into the Australian girls who told me that the next place looked good but they only had one hut and they were thinking about taking it.

I kept walking to find more "no vacancies" until I reached the last guesthouse at the end of the beach.

"We have a room. It's about five minutes walk back from the beach. Do you want to see it?" a slender Indian man asked.

I agreed to take a look and followed him on a dirt trail to what looked like a farmhouse. The room was fine--a light, a noisy overhead fan and a mattress pad on a brown wooden frame. I took it. It turned out to be a hot night where I was bitten and woken by mosquitoes.

The next morning I was up at dawn and headed out for a run and a swim. I then went to explore Om Beach. When I got over the hill, just on the north end of the beach, I found a nice looking place called the "Namaste."

I asked about rooms and a boy showed me the only vacancy, a thatch hut. The odor of mildew was so strong I couldn't take it for more than a minute. I asked if any other rooms would be available later that day. He told me he wasn't sure.

I went to further explore Om Beach. I decided at that point that if I didn't find a decent place to stay, I would leave the next day for North Goa.

After a swim, I went back to the "Namaste" and checked to see if any other rooms had become available. Nothing, in fact the hut I looked at earlier had even been taken. It was only about 9 a.m. and the sign on the wall read that the check out time was noon.

I had a feeling that a room would become available so I ordered a chai and a "lassi," a yogurt-shake, and waited. A young boy sat at the table and sold a couple of colorful necklaces of beads and shells to the staff. I had another chai and at 11 a.m. I saw a woman walk out with a bag.

I asked the man at the desk," Is she checking out?"

The man smiled and said no.

A few minutes later, another girl from the same group came out with a bag and I saw the guy with a key in his hand.

The man at the desk gave the boy a key and told him to show me the room. The boy told me, "Big room, this room, has bathroom, 300 rupees." We walked up a small hill to a nice little bamboo hut. Midnight blue tile steps led up to the door with a sign overhead that read, "Bambu House."

Inside, there was a sitting room with two wicker chairs and a little table. Green-leafed white curtains covered open-air criss-cross bamboo windows. The next room had a double bed and an oscillating fan set atop a wicker shelve stand.

There was even a bathroom with an Indian squat toilet, a faucet, a bucket and a drain in the floor. The room was nicely set on the side of the hill just overlooking the tops of green trees where a light breeze brought in the sound of waves unfolding on the seashore.

I thought, "Wow, if there is a time and a place to write, it's here and now."

# Dream Girl

It was in a sleeper car that I met her, Nathalie, a beautiful French Martiniquen princess. Her hair was black and curly, her skin was smooth and brown and her eyes were big and round. Her smile revealed her white teeth and happy, friendly disposition. We began to speak in the sleeper car when we realized that we would have a full day and second night on the train from Goa.

I was on my way to Delhi, and after a couple of days at my brother's place, I would move on to Dharamsala to attend the teachings of His Holiness the Dalai Lama. She was on her way to Agra, where after seeing the Taj Mahal was going to visit a hospital in a nearby town with the five other French nursing students she was traveling with.

We got along real well. Well, more than real well, there was chemistry in the air…strong chemistry. Nathalie taught me to play a French tarot card game and we played Chinese checkers with one of the other girls. We would talk for a while and then return to our books and exchange glances at one another. I was reading Richard's Bach's "One," and Nathalie was reading a book on prophecies.

It was around two a.m. when I woke to the girls shuffling about the sleeper car preparing to disembark and then everyone sat quietly waiting for the train to come to a halt. I was sure to get Nathalie's email address before we said goodbye and that same morning, in Delhi, I wrote her the following message:

*I find you extraordinarily beautiful*
*But it is the pull of our souls*
*That stirs my heart*

I used an online translator and sent it to her in French:

*Je vous trouve extraordinairement belle*
*Mais c'est la traction de nos ames*
*Qui remue mon Coeur*

She replied with the following:

*I am very touched by your message. I too have a few words for you.*

*The travel in the train with you was like a dream and it always will. And since my thinkings go freely to you, are they attracted by your peacefulness or your serenity?*

*I like your strange universe and the mysterious Varanasi seems ideal to meet you again.*

I chose the wrong train, the one that made stops throughout the night, but I still reached Varanasi in the morning. That's right, I chose my dream girl over the Dalai Lama.

I went to the parking lot and inquired about a rickshaw to the Ganpati Guesthouse where I had been once before. It was a very nice place situated at the edge of the old city right on the banks of the Holy River Ganga (commonly referred to as the Ganges in the west).

A large Indian man standing by the rickshaws pulled a business card out of his pocket and said that the Ganpati was his guesthouse. He went on to say that it was full and suggested I stay at the Yogi Lodge. I didn't recognize him from my prior visit and said that I would like to go check on my own. I asked to be dropped at the edge of Godualia, the old city, where I walked to the Ganpati.

The last time I was in Varanasi, I coined the phrase "Watch your step" as my mantra for the place. For one, when you enter the labyrinth of narrow walk streets of the old city it is easy to lose all sense of direction and get completely disorientated.

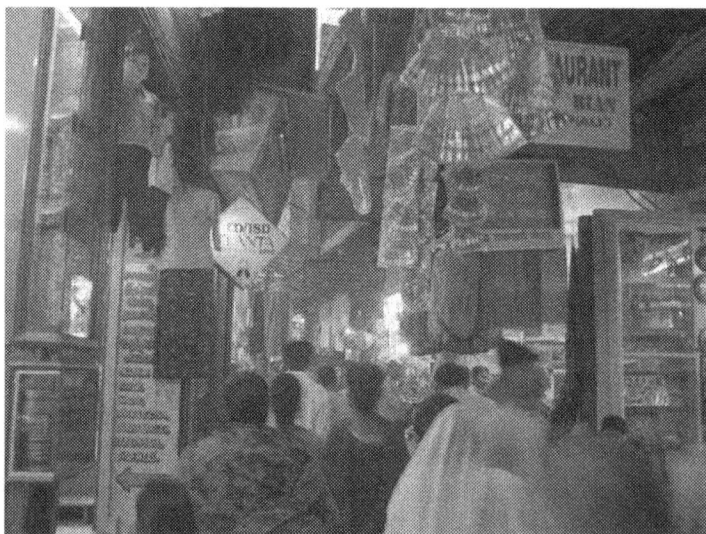

Two, there are cows and water buffalos everywhere and their droppings to avoid.

Three, the Ganga is lined with steps leading down to the water called "ghats."

And that's how I felt, immediately disorientated, but I made my way for the ghats and eventually came upon signs painted onto the sides of buildings for the Ganpati and neighboring hotels.

When I arrived at the front desk, I recognized the tall thin Indian man with dark wavy longish hair and a moustache and he recognized me from my prior visit. He asked me what room I had stayed in before. I pointed up to it, known as the big room, but he said it was occupied. He said he had an even better room on the next floor and had another guy take me to look at it. The room was nice, on the top floor with a balcony overlooking the Ganga and the courtyard.

I took it and relaxed for a while soaking up the view of the Ganga. Later, I went for a walk around Varanasi, also known as Benares, the city of lights. I bought candles and brightly colored fragrant flowers to warm up my room. In the afternoon, I phoned the number of the Sandaya Guesthouse that Nathalie sent me in an email. I told the man who answered the phone that I was trying to reach a guest there.

"What country?" he asked.

"France," I replied.

"Six girls?" he said.

"Yes, I would like to speak with Nathalie," I replied.

I went through a couple of French voices before I got to Nathalie and when she answered she asked, "Hello, police?"

"No, it's Sonny," I said.

"Where are you?" she asked.

"I'm here, Varanasi, Meer Ghat," I replied and asked, "I'd like to come to see you, can I come now?"
.
"Yes Sonny, come now," she answered.

As I walked along the river, I wondered why Nathalie had said "police" and was concerned and curious if something had happened. I asked directions that led me into the alleys of an area called Shivala and had some difficulty finding the Sandaya but eventually a bicycle rickshaw dropped me at the front door.

I walked into an open hallway at street level to find a couple of the girls waiting to use the pay phone and learned that one of them, Karine, had her bag stolen with her money, travelers checks, and flight ticket on the train to Varanasi. I was told that Nathalie had gone out, so we all went up to the room above and I waited.

A few minutes later, she arrived. We spoke in the crowded room with a little patio overlooking the busy street for a few minutes and then Nathalie suggested we go up on the rooftop to speak and enjoy the view.

The setting was perfect and I immediately felt a strong, seemingly mutual attraction. It was just becoming dark over the city of lights and after a few moments I said, "Do you want to kiss?"

Her first response was a little uncertain as I gave her a few soft kisses but after we talked about our meeting on the train, our feelings and our emails, she said she wanted to try the kiss again. This time it was "Wow," great, passionate.

From the rooftop, we saw that the other girls had arrived and taken a seat at a table at the terrace restaurant on the floor below us. We went down to join them and after the meal, the girls left, but Nathalie and I remained. We discussed what to do next.

"I don't want to be separated from you right now," Nathalie said.

I felt the same way and invited her to come to the Ganpati with me.

She packed a few of her things and just as we arrived at the street, a bicycle rickshaw rolled up dropping off two other foreigners who said that the rickshaw wallah was the best in Benares. A wallah is a person who performs a specific task, another example is a chai wallah: tea man…he is to tea what the barista is to espresso.

Indeed he was fast and Nathalie nicknamed him, "Speedy Gonzales." He dropped us at the main ghat where we set off down river for the Ganpati. The walk along the ghats was quiet, dark and a little eerie, yet at the same time, quite magical with Nathalie's hand clasped to mine.

We were lucky to find the gate at the Ganpati still open as it was around eleven p.m. and the posted time of closure was ten. We climbed the steps, and when we entered the room, I lit some candles illuminating the bright orange, fuchsia and white flowers I had bought earlier in the day and Nathalie said, "Sonny universe."

We sat on the balcony overlooking the river and just enjoyed being together before going to bed. In the morning, we woke up around five-thirty, in time to meet with the girls at the Sandaya for a Ganga boat excursion.

It was a beautiful morning and as we stepped down the ghats to the river, an orange sunrise sent a spectrum of light to the eyes reflected by the Ganga and its surroundings. The wooden boat looked river-worthy and luckily the seven of us along with the boatman fit just fine.

The boatman pulled us out onto the water with two wooden oars and rowed upstream past the laundry dhobis plying their trade of smacking dirt out of clothing on stone slabs lining the water's edge to the burning ghat. The burning ghat is of the holiest of crematoriums as the Ganga is said to cleanse away all sins and to die in Varanasi is said to ensure "Moksha," liberation, the release from the cycle of birth, death and rebirth.

He then pulled us out into the current and we drifted downstream along with the flickers of pinkish light dancing on the surface. He, like me, seemed to be in his glory, floating on the Ganga with this group of six French girls, not to mention the fare that a full boat would bring in.

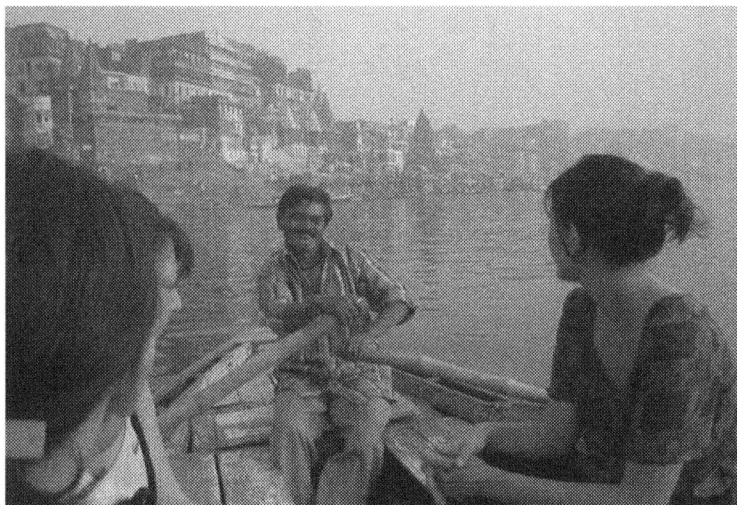

Downstream, we found the ghats teeming with the life and color of ritual bathing. Men and women washed and swam and prayed. This cleansing is the essence of Benares and the faith of the devout is seen in their practice.

Over the next few days, Nathalie and I became closer and closer. Perhaps it was the private serenade of tabla (a pair of two drums played with the hands to produce a vast array of sounds) and flute performed for us, or the strings of fragrant jasmine flowers I bought for Nathalie from the street vendors that I enjoyed to smell around her neck, or the rubbing of essential oils of musk, flowers, and opium onto each other at a shop in Godualia — or maybe it was Nathalie's soft kisses that woke me up in the night, or the astrologer who gave the lucky talisman (a magical charm) to Nathalie and prophesized a future of a passionate love life.

It could have been the evening at the Puja restaurant under the stars where an older couple told us their keys to a lasting relationship: share your feelings, be tender, and express your love and then they said, "J'taime" to each other and the English version, "I love you."

Well, one thing is for sure, and that is that Varanasi fell nothing short of magical!

Before we left, Nathalie decided to extend her stay in India after her tour of the south with the other girls. We took a wild auto-rickshaw ride over bumpy streets and through narrow corridors across town to the Air India office to change her flight and on the way back we stopped at a shop for a photocopy.

The shopkeeper, an older Indian man, looked suspiciously at Nathalie and I together and asked "Why?" inferring to the difference in the color of our skin.

Nathalie was quick to reply, "Love."

When we got back to the guesthouse, we packed up our things and then we held each other for a while before I had to go. I said goodbye to the other girls and Nathalie went with me to the railway station where I would board the Shiv-Ganga Express.

When we got to the platform, we kissed and I said, "J'taime," to Nathalie.

After another kiss, she whispered "J'taime aussi," in my ear.

But that wasn't it for Nathalie and me. I went on to meet her in Southern India, then she came with me to Delhi and we spent a couple of weeks traveling around the north together. Next, we took the train to Mumbai (also known as Bombay), where I saw her off for her return flight to France.

After a month of studying the language at Alliance Fran-
çaise in Delhi, I met Nathalie in Paris and we went on to
travel to Corsica and Italy together. After her holiday,
we spent blissful moments together in Annonay, a pleas-
ant town not far from Lyon where she tended to her
nursing studies.

Eventually, it was time for me to return to India, as I had
planned to join my family for a trip to Thailand for the
holidays. Nathalie and I spent our last night together
in Paris drinking red wine and eating fondue of cham-
pignons at the Taverne de Montmartre and later listening to a live jazz performance in a basement down the
street.

In the morning, I kissed her goodbye and while she lay
dreaming in bed, I boarded the underground metro at
Abbesses and went to catch the train to Charles De
Gaulle Airport where I boarded my flight to return to
India. From the air, I watched the French countryside
pass beneath me and dreamt of our next rendezvous.

.

# Act of God

The tsunami hit the west side of Phuket and we were on the east when it happened, at a marina with a hotel and residences. I was sitting by the pool reading a book on destinies when my brother came to give me the news. He had just returned from taking his newborn baby girl to the hospital for a "better be safe than sorry" sort of check up.

"A giant tsunami has hit Phuket, I guess Patong Beach has been wiped out."

I stood to watch water rushing into the slough leading into the marina along with boats full of day trip sightseers. The water kept coming and coming and so did the boats. We walked over to the bakery and saw that the section of the marina holding most of the boats appeared unaffected aside from the fish that were jumping out of the water, occasionally flopping onto the dock.

As I sat at an outside table and had some breakfast, a girl asked me if I knew where a payphone was that she could use. I offered to let her use my mobile. Her parents were at Ko Samui on the other side of mainland Thailand and she wanted to let them know she was all right.

She tried once but couldn't get through. I redialed the call about ten times before connecting to a hotel operator. She had stepped away so her friend took the phone and after trying to ring the room of the other girls' parents, she left a message, "Will you just tell them it's their daughter calling and we are O.K., we're safe, everything is O.K."

But for the Thai man standing at the railing across the walkway from me, everything was not O.K. He had received a call from the police saying that Phi Phi Don Island, where his family was, had been badly hit. He was unsure about their safety but had been told many people had climbed to higher ground. He hoped his family was among the safe.

We all sympathized with him still trying to put the pieces together on what had happened. "What a tragedy," one of the girls said. "I need to know what has happened," said the other. "Is there some place we can see an international news station in English, like BBC or CNN?"

Before I left to find my family, I wished the Thai man luck, "I hope you find your family, I hope they're well." He thanked me with a concerned look on his face.

I found my brother, his son, his girl-friend and baby daughter, my sister and her boyfriend, and my mother soaking up the sunshine at the hotel pool where it seemed almost as if nothing had happened aside from the stories my brother told that he heard from people he had spoken with.

One man was out at a little island nearest to the marina. It was a popular stop for the day trip sightseers to stop for a swim, to lounge or even snorkel, which was what he was doing. He was in the water with his wife and son when his boat captain called him in. Just as they climbed aboard, the surge came and the whole island was instantly submerged. The boat rode it without any problem.

The idea to see the news had seeped into my head by now and I returned to the room to turn on the television. The death toll was at 5,000. The tsunami had struck not only Thailand, but also India, Sri Lanka and originated from an earthquake centered off the coast of Indonesia.

I felt the earthquake that morning. So did my sister, she told her boyfriend to "Stop shaking the bed!" The whole place shook and not just for a moment but more like a continuous minute or two. I thought the shaking emanated from the room next to mine, as I've had active neighbors in the past.

At dinner, we vocalized some of the "what ifs?" that had been playing through our minds. For me, it was roll back 24 hours before the tsunami hit to Christmas day. My brother, my sister, her boyfriend and I were wading through a pitch-black cave with a flickering flashlight. My mother and nephew waited outside the caves opening to the sea at a small beach aside a high rising rock wall on an island in one of the hardest hit areas, Phang-Nga Bay. What if that wave would have hit then?

For my brother, it was the day before that. We were all at Patong Beach. What if it would've come while my mother had her eyes closed getting that Thai massage, while he and his son were riding jet skis, when nearly every chair on that beach was occupied with a life on holiday.

The next day I went with my brother and his son and rented a motorbike. I had thought it would be nice to find some way to help but we did like most everyone else we saw walking around in a mix of disbelief and shock. We rode toward Patong Beach. The traffic crawled up the hill where many people had taken refuge and then slowly down the other side where parked cars lined the road.

As we neared the beach, the disaster became evident. Two cars stood on end sandwiched to one another, roofs to destroyed businesses were caved in, and debris was piled high against a shrine of the Buddha. We walked out to the beach, not to the scene of sunny holidaymaking it was two days ago, but to a dismal scene of scattered wreckage. What happened to all those smiling faces that worked on the beach, the sun bed operators, masseuses, and fruit vendors?

We rode north along the western coastline past Kamala Beach to see more of the same and when we returned to our room we flipped on the television for the latest update. The death toll was up to 50,000 and rising. The whole thing was so sad and so difficult to believe. It was as if it were all just one big elaborate act. Unfortunately, for far too many, it was all too real.

# Personal Vehicle

Taking the train seemed to be the more rational choice for comfort and safety. That's why I had a train ticket in hand the night before I left. However, it could also be limiting as to what I might encounter and as I packed my bags, I thought, "I had always envisioned this trip to be a motorbike adventure into the Indian Himalaya."

In the morning, I loaded my bags onto the Indian made Royal Enfield 350cc Bullet. The bike was only a year and half old but an Enfield Bullet is a classic design. I zigzagged my way out of Delhi and then puttered up the road avoiding the slow moving ox carts and oncoming trucks and busses to Rishikesh situated at the foothills of the Himalaya along the banks of the Holy Ganga River.

In Rishikesh, I checked-in to the Sivananda Ashram and on the roof of the guesthouse I met an older Indian couple enjoying the fresh air and valley view.

When I told them that I had come by motorbike, the woman asked, "Why didn't you just take the train?"

"Those bus driver's are murderers," said the man.

"I nearly did, but the bike gives me greater freedom to explore the mountains," I replied.

I took a day trip up river playing Ganga River motorbike taxi, picking up a couple of passengers and dropping them at their destinations. Other than that, the bike remained parked for the duration of my six-day stay.

When I went to the ashram reception to checkout, the receptionist asked me to give him a lift into town to another ashram where he was going to attend a lecture on Vedanta, the ancient philosophy of India, which literally translates to Ved – knowledge and anta – the end, the end of knowledge.

He sat sidesaddle with his orange robe fluttering in the wind and as we rolled into town he asked me where I was going. I told him I was going to Dharamsala, which is quite a distance.

"The Dalai Lama is there," he said and asked, "Why do you take your personal vehicle?"

"If I hadn't, I wouldn't have had the pleasure of giving you a lift into town," I replied.

As there were very few road signs and most of them were written in Sanskirt text, it was necessary to ask my way to each destination.

If in doubt, I pulled over and asked, "Chandigarh?" to the nearest bystander, who would then point me along my way.

This is road navigation Indian style. Even the best map is only a rough guide. You must ask.

I passed a guy pushing his bike on the side of the road and pulled over to ask what his problem was.

"Puncture," he said and continued rolling his bike.

"Oh, I was going to offer you petrol," I said pointing to the bottle I had in the rack.

"What if I got a puncture, where, when, what would I do? I don't have any kind of spare," I thought.

Having had ridden a long day and still not reaching Chandigarh, I found myself asking the question, "Why did I have to take the motorbike, if I were on the train I would be sitting comfortably reading a book and drinking a chai?"

Finding a room in Chandigarh was a challenge, but when I did, I washed the black road grime of dust and exhaust from my face and went for a dinner of pizza and a veg kathi roll. The guys at the hotel were very accommodating and insisted I park the Royal Enfield in the lobby where it would be safe.

I got an early start at seven in the morning and shot out of town before the roads got too busy. I planned a route that the map indicated as being a major highway for at least half the journey and seemed the easiest to navigate. For the first stretch of highway I was going to take the direction of Bilaspur and then Manali.

I had just made a turn four kilometers back when I stopped to top off my petrol. The station attendant asked where I was going and when I told him Dharamsala, he said if I take the Bilaspur direction it would be one hundred kilometers further than if I went back four kilometers and continued in the direction of Una. He showed me his suggested route on my map. I took his advice and turned back.

It wasn't long and I even saw a sign for Dharamsala. I continued along occasionally checking my route with a roadside bystander and passed through the town of Ananpur Sahib and over a bridge where at a roundabout I went right, as a prior directional sign had indicated, but soon found myself on a narrow single lane road.

I asked a group of men standing around outside a shop in the small village, "Una?" They pointed me to continue on, take a left and follow the road back to the highway.

I took the left and rolling down a hill into a small green valley I felt the bike wobble and realized my tire was deflating.

Just as I rolled to a halt, a man passing me on a bicycle stopped. He didn't speak much English and I don't speak much Hindi but he communicated to me that he would ride his bike to the mechanic and send him to me. I agreed to wait. Thunder roared and it began to drizzle.

A few minutes had passed and another guy stopped and offered to help. I told him someone was coming.

"Nobody's coming," he said and suggested I push the bike to a mechanic.

He'd help me.

Just after we had removed the screw that had made the puncture from the tire, the man on the bicycle returned.

"Mechanic coming, two minutes," he said.

"I guess there is someone coming," said the other guy.

A couple of boys showed up on a scooter. They removed the wheel from the frame of the bike and rode away with it. They left me an umbrella that I put over my bags in order to protect them from the increasingly heavy rain.

The man on the bicycle said, "Problem solved," and asked me for a hundred rupees. In fact, the problem wasn't solved yet, but the solution was in progress.

"Koy batne," I said and gave it to him, "Koy batne" is Hindi for "No problem."

He pedaled away and there I sat with the Royal Enfield Bullet, my bags strapped to it, an umbrella covering the bags and the rear wheel gone amidst a green valley in God knows where India.

The thunder continued to roar and the rain continued to pour and I thought to myself as if it were rumbling from the sky, "Adventure you wanted, adventure you'll get."

The boys returned and said, "Finished," holding up the dead tire tube, "Market, two hundred rupees."

"OK," I agreed and off to the market they went.

Just as they returned with the repaired wheel the man on the bicycle rode up. The boys picked up the rear of the bike and replaced the wheel. I settled up with the mechanic for three hundred rupees, the equivalent of about seven U.S. dollars or six euro, inclusive of tube and labor.

Before I could get back on the road, the man on the bicycle invited me to his house for tea.

"Only ten minutes," he said.

His smiling wife greeted us as we rode up. We went into the small brick house, drank tea and crunched on a little fried snack that was in the shape of a wheel. She offered me lunch and I was happy to accept the tasty meal of roti, a tortilla like bread, some green vegetables, a soup of peas and potatoes and pickled green mangoes.

I thanked them for the meal and they invited me to return. We walked out of the house and as the man showed me his two goats, their daughter and one of their two sons arrived home from school. I told the girl that her mother was a very good cook and her father helped me with my bike, although I don't know how much of it she understood. Villagers looked curiously at me as I rolled out the alley onto the street and within a few minutes I was back on the highway.

I had been back on the road for less than an hour when I heard a rattling noise coming from the rear of the bike. I pulled over and tightened my bags and continued on. The rattling continued. I checked it again and found the chain guard cracked where it attached near the rear sprocket. With every bump, which there were many, it rattled and clanged. I pulled over again and bought a single cigarette. As I lit it, I looked across the street to see sparks.

I crossed the street and said to an older man sitting in a chair reading the newspaper, "I just realized that my chain guard was cracked and looked over and saw this shop."

"You want welding?" he asked.

"Yes," I replied.

Within a couple minutes, the boys sparked up the chain guard and it was ready to go.

"Five rupees," one of the boys said.

The road split and split again.

To avoid any confusion I asked at every junction, "Dharamsala?"

After passing a nice looking guesthouse perched on a hillside overlooking a grand valley, I pulled over to the side of the road and considered calling it a day but when I looked to find the time was only two-thirty in the afternoon I decided to press on.

I continued through rolling hills and kept climbing more and more into the mountains. Just as a few drops of rain began to fall, I saw a sign for a rest house a few kilometers ahead.

The few drops became many and I stopped to ask how far away the rest house was.

"Sot kilometers," a boy said, sot is Hindi for seven.

Thunder exploded, and we exchanged speechless wide-eyed looks at each other.

The many drops became a full-on downpour. As I rode with my head down, I watched the wheels slowly turn on the odometer. I felt the water in my shoes, my pants, and everything was getting soaked.

When my seven kilometers were up, at a fork in the road I asked, "Rest house?" to a man at a corner shop.

He pointed to a small uphill road that I had just passed with a small sign, "REST HOUSE, tourist welcome to stay."

I rode up the hill, quickly parked, removed my bags and carried them up some stone steps to find a group picnicking on the porch under the cover of the rest house.

First, I asked the wrong guy, "Room?"

"No," he answered.

But then, when he left with the group, I figured out who the caretaker was and when I asked, "Room?"

He showed me a simple room with a double bed and attached bath. The rest house had only two guest rooms joined by a common sitting room in the middle.

I took it, and after changing out of my wet clothes, I warmed up with a cup of tea and went outside for a look around. The rain had ceased to a few stray drops and from the top of the hill I could see a beautiful view of lush green fields, trees, hills and slate roofs.

After a decent meal and a good night's sleep, I woke to the sounds of heavy rain and thunder. Instead of packing for another day's journey, I sat in the room and read.

Later, I took a stroll down to the road and found the caretaker joking around with a laughing chai wallah. As I tilted a hot cup of chai with one hand and warmed the other over a glowing fire, I laughed with the locals over our mix of English and Hindi and thought, "I sure am happy I didn't take the train."

# Fortune Cookie

It was the message in a fortune cookie that brought me to India for the first time. I went to see my brother and coincidently the timing worked out that His Holiness the Dalai Lama was giving his annual public teachings in Dharamsala.

My brother Jake had planted the seed while we spent Christmas together in my mother's living room. I had given the book, "The Art of Happiness" co-authored by the Dalai Lama as a gift.

"I've heard that the Dalai Lama lives in the mountains of Northern India not far from Delhi," he said.

I had been reading books by the Dalai Lama and had developed an interest in his teachings. I remember the first time he caught my attention. It was on a television program where he spoke of compassion and non-violence. He said he would rather allow a mosquito to suck his blood than smash it on his arm.

Then there was a book where he explained the principle teachings of the Buddha, called the four noble truths, which essentially say that desire is the root cause of suffering and that the path leads to the cessation of desire and therefore leads to the reduction of suffering and true happiness.

It was in Delhi that I boarded my first Indian train for my first India adventure. I entrusted it to my brother and his assistant who only booked me about halfway to a small town called Kalka, where I arrived at twilight, and got a taxi through what appeared to be some sort of taxi union auction.

I was wide-eyed and as we sped along the country roads the sun came up. I saw all kinds of things; there were gatherings of people parading in the streets and pilgrimages to temples up steep mountain paths, children threw colored powder at the car as we passed them on the road. It was a festival day called "Holi," and one of the biggest of the year, celebrated all over India.

In Dharamsala, I continued to get dowsed with color and by the time I finally settled into a room I was covered in "Holi." The room had an unattached shower with only cold water and I thought, "If years of meditation won't wake you up, this cold shower will."

The Tibetan Ashoka guesthouse was in McLeod Ganj, considered to be Upper Dharamsala, and about a kilometer
above the Dalai Lama's residence and temple. McLeod Ganj
straddles a ridge in the Himalayan foothills with tremen-
dous views in all directions. The place teamed with the ma-
roon robes and shaved heads of monks along with Tibetan
refugees, national resident Indians and foreign visitors from
around the globe.

The teachings based on the "Bodhisattva Way of Life" com-
menced the following day. A Bodhisattva is the Tibetan
(Mahayana) Buddhist ideal; one who has attained bodhicitta
(bodhi-wakefulness, citta-consciousness) with the cultiva-
tion of compassion by exchanging oneself for others.

I began the day with Tibetan herbal tea and brown bread in a café where I met a friendly couple that was also on their way to the teachings. They told me that people were already going to the temple to reserve their places to sit. When we arrived we found the ground covered with "reserved" signs.

Eventually, we took a seat in the aisle-way that His Holiness the Dalai Lama would enter through. Lamas wearing pointy hats and blowing horns that sounded like oboes preceded him. He looked around and waved to the crowd with a smile on his face that exuded friendship.

Monks continued to chant as he took his seat, and then he joined in. When he began to speak in Tibetan, I attempted to tune my radio to the English translation being simultaneously broadcast, but was unable to get it. I was lucky to find someone playing a large radio aloud to a gathering of other English listeners sitting on some steps towards the back of the temple grounds.

The Dalai Lama spoke on the ideals of the Bodhisattva and the importance of learning with the heart as well as the head, development of the altruistic mind, and the desire to attain enlightenment for the sake of all sentient beings.

Exiting the temple was a squeeze with all of the monks in red robes flowing out the gate as if pouring from a ketchup bottle. Outside, women sold a variety of Tibetan snacks, and the road was lined with all kinds of Tibetan wares; prayer beads, monk's bags, seating cushions, jewelry, shawls and clothing.

The second time I saw the Dalai Lama was in Darjeeling. He spoke on "The Thirty-Seven Practices of the Bodhisattva" to an overwhelmingly large crowd of Tibetan refugees who were so happy he was coming that they had lined the road with one welcome banner after the next.

The third time I went to see him, I rode a motorbike through the snow to reach McLeod Ganj where he spoke on "The Great Stages of the Path."

On my first visit to India, after ten days of teachings, I returned to Delhi to meet up with my brother. We went on to travel in Asia for another two weeks and then he temporarily quit his job and we flew back to the States together via a quick stop in Amsterdam.

He had been working for a burgeoning technology company in Delhi but was having a difficult time. He worked very long hours and kept getting ill from food poisoning. My mother had told me of his condition the day I cracked open the fortune cookie that I received with my dinner from Mao's Chinese Kitchen on Pacific Avenue in Venice. I unfolded the small piece of paper and read, "Somebody needs your help."

# Ganga Gurus

Swami Sivananda was a key propagator of Yoga and Vedanta and the Sivananda Ashram in Rishikesh interested me for the study thereof. When I arrived, I was given The Divine Life Society Daily Programme that specified a yoga class followed by a lecture on philosophy. "Perfect," I thought.

The next morning, I set out early at 6:10 but a little late to find the yoga class by 6:15.

When I asked the few souls wandering the ashram at that hour, "Do you know where the yoga class is?"

No one seemed to know.

I returned to my room and enjoyed a cup of tea before setting out to find the lecture on philosophy. On the way down from my room I met a guy, Scott, who was from Seattle in the stairwell.

When I asked, "Do you know where the philosophy lecture is?"

He said, "Come on, I'll show you, that's where I'm going."

We walked down the hill and when we arrived I saw "Yoga Hall" painted on the exterior wall of the building with the class times.

"So this is where the yoga classes are," I said.

"Yeah, it's too bad they're not having it right now," Scott replied.

We climbed the steps and waited on the veranda overlooking the Ganga. A suspension footbridge, named Ram Jhula (God Bridge), joins the banks lined with ashrams and ghats leading down to the water.

Scott noticed a small bird repeatedly flying into a mirrored glass window on the exterior of the room. He walked over and waved his hand in the air shooing the bird away from the window before we entered the lovely room with hardwood floors and windows revealing the green hills surrounding us. As the class settled in, I observed a large man with a clean-shaven head, dressed in orange, sitting peacefully as students shut the windows behind him to block off the noise from the ghats below.

He began by commenting on the bird that had returned to the window. He likened the bird that kept running it's beak into the glass to the human condition of searching for our selves within our ego and that the ego is an illusion just like the reflection of the bird in the mirrored glass. He compared the ego with waves on the ocean.

"You are not a wave, you are the water," he said.

After the talk, I still sought to find myself in a good yoga class. However, with the word "yoga" meaning "union," between one's individual consciousness and the Universal Consciousness, perhaps I should say I already attended a good yoga class in the philosophy lecture.

But like many, I am using "yoga" to refer to physical yoga or hatha yoga where the practice of positioning the body in various postures, called asanas, along with proper breathing, pranayama, and concentration has great benefits such as increased flexibility, awareness, and relaxation which can all contribute to realizing the goal of "union" with the Divine.

I made a series of inquiries but it wasn't until the following morning that I found out that the open yoga class at the Sivananda Ashram had been suspended. So I sat at the ghats and took in the Ganga and two chais before I ascended the steps for the philosophy lecture.

Swamiji began the lecture with a series of jokes, "Why not to mess with children." After the room broke into laughter several times, he said it was his point to reveal our true nature, happiness. He then spoke of attraction and repulsion and said "I am" in the voices of a cow and then a chicken.

"Could you eat a cow that mooed, "I am" to you?" he asked.

The class was dismissed and outside on the veranda Scott approached me and said, "I have a good example of attraction and repulsion. I found the girl sitting in front of me attractive and smiled at her. She shook her head and made a face. That's repulsion."

I went in search of my yoga class and ended up sitting in a group at the feet of a yogi across the river at the Vedniketan Ashram. He had long dark hair and a bushy gray beard. He spoke of "Prana," intelligent life force energy, in a room filled with photos of gurus and yogis.

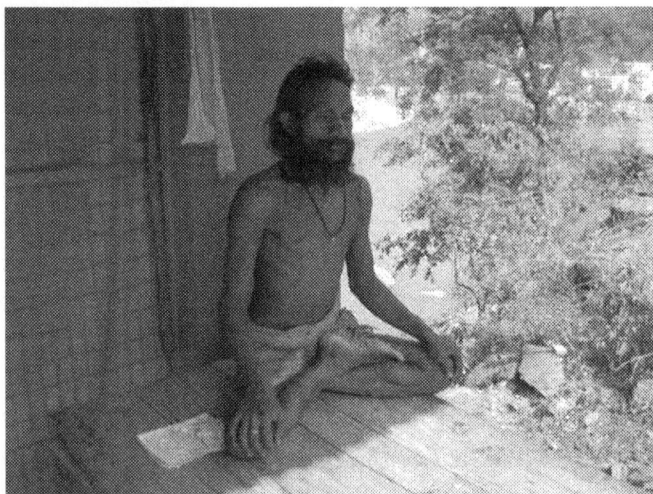

He claimed that Hindu philosophy and yogis have known for ages what modern western science is only beginning to understand.

"If Stephen Hawking would only read Hindu philosophy, he would have everything figured out," he said.

At the end of the class he went over some rules of the ashram.

"Please do not bring anyone from outside the ashram to your rooms, especially chillum smoking babas," he said.

A chillum is like a pipe used to smoke hashish and a baba is a wandering holy man on a spiritual quest who is also known as a sadhu.

He made the voice of a girl and said, "I never wanted to have children in New York but now that I'm in India…."

And then went on to say, "Chillum smoking babas are the easiest way to get pregnant."

Later, I returned to the Vedniketan for a hatha yoga class. It was held in a large hall in the middle of the ashram grounds. A wall was lined with shelves of scattered books. I arrived two minutes late and immediately grabbed a mat and began to stretch and contort my body. The instructor was a young Indian guy who ran a fast class and said most everything in threes.

"Focus, focus, focus" and "Relax, relax, relax."

I returned to the Sivananda Ashram for the evening Sat-sanga. I sat in the Samadhi Shrine lined with paintings and writings of Swami Sivananda. There was singing and chanting from the Bhagavad-Gita (the classic story where good conquers evil with the aid of Lord Krishna as charioteer in the battle) and then a distinguished looking man wrapped in white spoke of the Vedas (ancient Indian philosophical truths) and the Divine. The day was concluded with prayers and blessings of long life.

As for my life, India is like the university I had always hoped to find, where you step away from western convention and feel as if you are reinventing learning itself, but in fact, are only making small discoveries of what is ancient and ageless. You take the time to speak with the sadhus, beggars, and chai wallahs or anyone who may stop you in your path. Because in India, everywhere you turn there is a lesson.

# Steps

I stepped over the bridge to platform three at the Delhi Cantonment Railway Station where I stood sipping hot chai from a clay cup. As I awaited the Shatabdi Express, I looked across the tracks to a pinkish Hindu temple with a tall phallic tower jetting into the sky. In India, I have come to accept that everything is holy; holy river, holy temple, holy mountains, holy cow and this journey was taking me to the holy lake of Pushkar in India's state of Rajasthan.

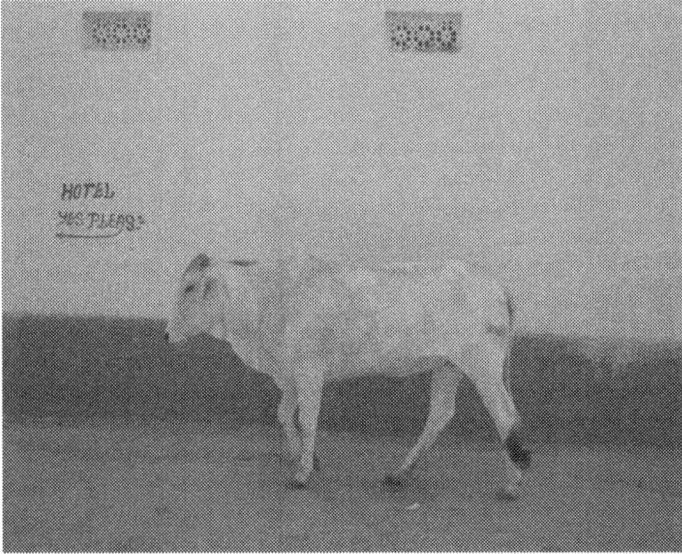

A train rolled in on platform two. A man standing in an open doorway of the passing train waved to a little girl holding hands with an older man standing on the platform before it came to a stop.

In the next moment, from the other direction, came the Shatabdi Express. I quickly stepped up into the red and yellow air-conditioned train car and walked along the red floor beneath fans that dangled from the ceiling and a fluorescent tube illuminating the aisle. The seats were two-tone brown and curtains of muted red checkerboard hung bunched by the windows.

After a breakfast of vegetable cutlet with bread, I closed my eyes for a while. When I opened them, I enjoyed watching the passing stillness of the hot desert flora.

The train reached Ajmer in the early afternoon where I stepped down. The station was bustling with men in fresh looking long white shirts and white trousers wearing close fitting black caps reminding me that Ajmer is a holy place of pilgrimage for Muslims.

Outside the station, I was accosted by an onslaught of taxi and rickshaw drivers. But who can blame them, they are only trying to make a living, do their duty, play their role. I walked through the crowd and jumped into a passing multi-passenger motor-rickshaw for two rupees to the Pushkar bus stand.

I bought my ticket and a bag of peanuts and stepped up to the half-full, half empty bus. I shared a seat near the back with a local woman decorated in Rajasthani red textiles and silver jewelry around a face that told tales of years gone by. I cracked open the peanuts and tossed the shells out of the window as we climbed the brown mountainside.

Reaching Pushkar, I was greeted by the usual hotel touts.

"Room, swimming pool, air-conditioning, nice view," they plied.

Even though I showed no interest, one of the guys continued working on me as I walked down the road.

"Just come take a look," he pleaded.

When I tried speaking only French, he added that he had French girls staying at his hotel. I laughed, and eventually, he too disappeared.

At the road that circled the lake, I turned left passing by the shopkeepers that said, "Hello," and "Take a look my shop."

Halfway around the lake, I went to check out the Lotus Hotel for a room. It was a shanti (meaning peaceful) place with great views overlooking the lake surrounded by ghats and whitewashed temples and palaces. I found the doorway closed and locked.

"Finished," said a white-haired Indian man sitting beneath a magnificent bodhi tree.

I continued around the lake until I found an alley that led to the lake. I sat on the ghats and rested in the shade of a whitewashed wall. A Brahman (Priest) splashed a bucket of water onto a lone tree that rose from a square of earth surrounded by the cement of the ghats leading down to the lake, where he sprinkled seed for birds.

I found my place at the Bharatpur Palace, where I chose room number two as its' conductivity to the lake breeze was well demonstrated to me. The room was small, square and cell-like with bars and inward opening wooden doors for windows looking out over the lake in two directions and a basic double bed. It was pure simplicity.

That evening, I wandered through the market and then through an archway down to the ghats. Before I entered, I bought a mix of flowers from a young woman sitting beneath the archway. As I walked down the steps, I heard a man leaning out of a window overhead shout, "Ram, Ram."

Sitting quietly, I took in the magic and splendor of the place before I stepped down to the water's edge. Pujas (prayers) were being performed all around the lake. To my left, a Brahman made puja with voice and fire. Behind him, a woman draped in red stood still with her hands pressed together. As bells rang out, birds took flight over the oasis.

The next morning, I woke up feeling refreshed, lucid and light in the little cell with the lake breeze and views in two directions. Out the windows, the sun shone, the birds flew and people rejoiced all around the lake.

I decided to visit the quiet ghat where the tree rose out of the square. On my way down to the lake, I passed a man sitting in the shade of the tree. At the lake's edge, I sprinkled flowers of fuchsia and yellow that sat floating on the holy water.

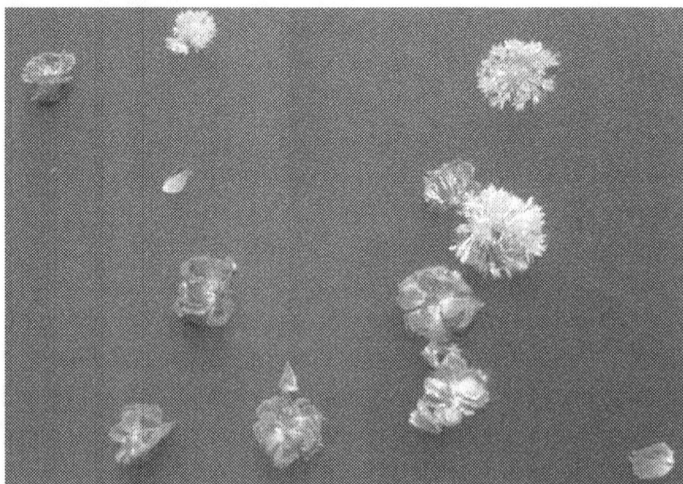

When I walked back up, we both said "Namaste," which in India is commonly used as "Hello" but is also translated as "The divine in me recognizes the divine in you."

He invited me to sit with him. His white-gray hair was slicked back away from his friendly eye-glassed face. He wore a white tank top and a plaid lungi (like a sarong, worn by men). He told me a story of the lake that appeared when Brahma (the Hindu Creator God) dropped a lotus flower in its place.

"Many people come here to worship God," he said and imparted, "All the same God, one God."

From the lake, I ascended to the Savrita Temple, named for Brahma's wife. It was a hot walk, but well worth the views from the path where the wind swept around the golden brown mountain cooling the sweat on my body.

After my morning adventures, I returned to the peace of my Zen cell on the lake. I took a cleansing shower and relaxed wrapped in a simple white lungi in the shanti spot. My mind felt clear and my body refreshed.

I packed my bag and split. I stopped for a veg sandwich and enjoyed some conversation and a chai with an Italian couple and a guy from Zambia. I lost track of time until I realized I only had fifty minutes to board my train in Ajmer for the journey back to Delhi.

I was lucky to step up into the bus from Pushkar to Ajmer just as it was pulling away and a ten-rupee auto rickshaw ride put me at the railway station with time to spare. I was again reminded that Ajmer was a holy place for Muslims when a friendly man dressed in white with a small black cap smiled and said hello as I boarded the train.

From my seat in the air conditioned chair car, I reflected on the lotus flower lake said to have been created by the Hindu God Brahma where I sat with the man who said, "The One God, all the same God." I thought of the Muslim man with the friendly smile and of the message of Islam, "The Creator of the world is One," and of a teaching I attended given by His Holiness the Dalai Lama where he said, "Everything is interconnected and interrelated."

# Return to the Source

"Road closed," said the man at the ticket window to my request for a bus ticket to Gangotri where I planned to begin the nineteen kilometer walk to Gaumukh, the recognized source of India's Holy River Ganga. He suggested I return the next day and try again.

I walked along the dirt road lined with busses and then alongside a small stream and through the alleys of Rishikesh to the main road, turned left and walked toward Ram Jhula. It was early morning and pilgrims, mostly young Indian men dressed in orange, were making their way to the river any way they could, some by foot and some loaded into and piled on top of auto-rickshaws, cars, and trucks.

I slipped out of the steady stream of foot traffic walking up the path to the bridge and went for a chai by the riverside. The Ganga was blanketed by a celestial mist softening the view of spots of orange moving around the ghats on the other side of the river. "Bum Bum" and "Bum Bhole" they chanted in praise to Lord Shiva, who is said to have caught the Ganga in his matted locks in order to cushion its earthly impact when it descended from heaven.

I spent the day along the Ganga and then took a room next to the bus stand for the night. I was up at dawn and when I asked, "Gangotri?" to the man at the ticket window he replied, "No bus to Gangotri," but told me to return for a bus to Uttarkashi from where I could continue on.

When I arrived in Uttarkashi, I was greeted by drivers at the taxi stand along a road lined with buildings of cement swiss cheese. Gaping holes had been created by large boulders that must have come from the "mountain-slide" across the road.

"Gangotri?" they asked.

"Yes." I said.

"Come."

It wasn't until the next morning that we departed after a night's rest at a guesthouse near the gurgling river. The driver was full of intent and I felt confident that he would deliver us. Passengers took quick rides standing on the rear bumper as we rode from village to village in the full jeep until we stopped behind a long string of vehicles awaiting a landslide to be cleared from the road.

A few hours and a few sticks of dynamite later we were back on the move and arrived safely in Gangotri.

The path from the taxi stand was lined with restaurants and shops selling all kinds of pilgrimage goods.

I bought a wool shawl, a hat and a music cassette that caught my ear with an exuberant, "Bum Bhole."

I started up the path in the morning after visiting the temple where I was touched with red paste on the forehead by a priest.

A sadhu tempted me to stop for a chai and I spoke briefly with a man from India's state of Punjab but continued on. The many voices of "Bum Bhole, Bum Bum, and Jai Bhole," became a single symphony elevating the nature of the trip and reminding me to keep my focus on the source.

I climbed through the landscape of pine trees and rocky cliffs and then over white rushing streams that fed the Ganga before I made my first rest stop about ten kilometers in. After another five kilometers, I passed the line of chai stands overlooking the few scattered buildings and tents of Bhojwasa below.

I began to tire and sat for a rest in an open lunar landscape of rock until I was encouraged by a friendly Indian couple to continue on; "That's it," the man said as he pointed, "That's the tip of the glacier, the source, Gaumukh."

Up a little further, people bathed in the ice-cold water where just one dip is said to cleanse away all sins and purify the soul. A sadhu maintained a shrine of bells hanging from poles wrapped in shiny gold and red threads around the image of Lord Shiva. Orange, yellow, and red flags mixed in the sky with white snow-capped peaks.

Just around the bend stood the archway of marbled ice where the river begins its visible journey. "Gaumukh" translates to "Cow's mouth," and the cow is a twenty-something kilometer long glacier. Within it, the Ganga is formed.

Three young Indian men urged me to come closer. I stood a stone's throw away when massive chunks of ice plummeted from the archway into the water splashing waves in all directions.

The force of the river spread the bluish-white ice boulders downstream like an avalanche. The hands of the young men held a cube between them as if it were a precious gem emanating life force energy.

I returned to Bhojwasa for a night's rest and in the morning stood outside the doorway of the guesthouse taking in the sunrise against the magnificent scenery waiting to see which way the wind would blow. Would I continue on to Tapovan, a steep four kilometers up over the glacier from Gaumukh where it was suggested I go with a guide, would I return to the source and explore the surrounding area, or would I walk back down to Gangotri?

A passing sadhu looked at me and said, "Tapovan?"

It only took me a moment to settle my bill and grab my bag. I found the black-bearded orange-turbaned sadhu freshening up at a cascading stream just off the path. I waited a few minutes and then together we walked.

We made a few stops; one at the tent of a white-bearded baba, the next was to talk with a lovely occidental couple on their way down from Tapovan who spoke of mountain goats and wildflowers, and then the holy dipping hole.

It was from there that the ascent began, up, around, and over the top of the glacier.

"Slowly, slowly," my guide said as we stopped to catch our breath.

We sat on rocks over the mix of ice and sand where he removed his worn-out sandals and showed me the badly cracked soles.

I had a good pair of comfortable sandals with soft leather uppers and tire tread-like soles slipped into the side pocket of my pack I offered to the sadhu. They were a perfect fit. He happily accepted and left his behind. When I followed him and the imprints of my own sandals, I felt as if I were following in my own footsteps.

"Which way Baba?" a guide with a man and a woman asked as we passed blue ice craters and approached the most vertical portion of the climb.

He pointed up. I looked to see some other climbers high above. We only took ten or twenty steps at a time before stopping to look down at what we had covered.

Up, up we went until we reached a level plane overlooking the glacier where we all sat and took in the atmosphere. The young guide enjoyed the words of the sadhu, laughing and exclaiming, "Good Baba." From that time forward, I thought of him as "Acha Baba." Acha means good in Hindi.

The wind urged us to move on with an accomplice, dust. The terrain suddenly changed from jagged, tan-colored rocks into a verdant boulder strewn valley. We followed a small path to soon arrive at a house of stones built into the hillside.

We took a seat on a blanket the baba laid out on the ground outside the front door. People came and went but we sat there all afternoon under the changing sky of blue and fast moving white clouds with the young guide and a young boy that stayed and worked at the house. The temperature went from hot to cold depending on the wind and intensity of the sun.

The boy's foot was twisted inward with his toes pointed toward his opposite ankle but he seemed capable of getting around with apparent ease and the handicap didn't seem to impair his natural joyous quality. He seemed fascinated with the baba and we all smiled and laughed together facing the holy Mount Shivling in Tapovan, which literally translates to "meditation jungle," where yogis have come for ages to realize their true nature.

Just before dinner, mountain goats descended onto the camp and competed to lick mineral deposits from a rock by bucking their way into prime positions with the use of large crescent-shaped horns. We filled the small front room of the house of stones for a meal of dahl (lentils), rice and chapatti (tortilla-like bread).

In the back room beneath an overhanging slab of rock that the house was built into, we slept like sardines in a can, and in the morning were woken with a hot chai in the hand. It was a nice touch to begin the day with.

The baba had slept in the front room and with the help of an interpreter came to tell me he would be going down today and asked if I would come along. I told them that I would remain in Tapovan. When we emerged from the cave-like room, we discovered a beautiful day of clear blue sky.

I stepped off to explore the valley passing by another stone house and a sadhu making puja before descending into a calm green meadow divided by the crystalline "Sky Ganga" stream. I walked along a lightly worn path where mountain wildflowers sprung from the earth.

I spotted my own footsteps and tracked "Acha Baba" to another house built into the rocks at the edge of the valley plane where we shared our last chai together that was heated by the sun. It was quite ingenious, a ring of mirrors directed onto a pressure cooker hanging in the center. And then, he left, back down the path.

I returned to the room beneath the rock slab for a rest and when I got up, I found a young smiling woman with longish sandy blonde hair sitting in the main room. She introduced herself as Talei, an Australian doctorate student of tabla, studying in Mumbai.

A tall muscular man with a shaved head, Talei's boyfriend Brett, joined us. When Talei left the room to take a nap, Brett and I continued to talk. He was quite impressed to hear that I had worked on Hollywood movies and thought it must have been difficult to leave such a career behind.

He related it to his own experience.

His friends had said, "You have a great job, you get a company car, a BMW, you make good money and you drive around with the upper echelon of society."

He was a BMW car salesman.

"Why would you want to leave such a career?"

The question seemed foreign to me. It never seemed as if I had much of a choice, it just happened, and now, Tapovan felt like the "Upper echelon."

They invited me to go for a walk up to a lake that their guide had told them about. As we walked, I told them of the mountain goats we had seen the prior day. Brett got quite excited and said that he had a real affinity for goats, as his zodiac sign is Capricorn.

We climbed the rugged hillside and jumped from boulder to boulder to the edge of the turquoise blue lake. From the high vantage point we could see the width but not the breadth of the glacier, the brown-sided mountains, the white-capped mountains, and the green valley but no sign of Brett's celestial siblings.

Back at the stone house, the man and boy of the house along with another man whom I had met over at the house of solar chai were all sitting together listening to music from an old cassette tape player when I recalled that I had the cassette I purchased down in Gangotri in my bag.

I dug it out and gave it to the boy who quickly removed the cellophane wrapping. He and the older man of the house inspected the cover of the tape. The older man pointed to a photo and said, "Very good man."

The boy dropped the cassette in and hit play. The Indian music filled the air. The boy studied the cover and bounced his head along with the beat. The man from the house of solar chai assumed a cross-legged sitting position just in front of the speaker. My favorite song began to play with the exuberant "Bum Bhole." When they heard it, everyone's eyes lit up.

We were all really getting into the music and singing the "Bum Bhole's" together when Brett and Talei stepped into the house. It was the perfect song for this sacred place of Shiva sitting beneath Mount Shivling and Brett and Talei called me, "The DJ to the Himalayas."

After both sides of the cassette were played and it began again, the batteries fizzled out making for very slow songs. The Indian men began to play cards and Brett and Talei joined in. I stepped out into the meditation jungle and took a seat atop a precipice overlooking the valley of the Ganga, both fluid and frozen.

I got up and was walking back along the ridge when I spotted the goats feeding below me along the hillside. I immediately thought of Brett and quickly went to get him but arrived just as the evening meal was being served.

After we ate, we set out to see the goats but were too late, they had gone. We decided to continue walking along the ridge, but still, no goats. We dropped down into a chasm of wildflowers and then up another ridge toward the meadow where the "Sky Ganga" stream flows.

As a mist of fog blew in, the light diminished. We decided it would be wise to turn back and follow the low path from the chasm of flowers.

Brett got ahead of me as I occasionally stopped to listen to the silence for any sound of movement on the rocks.

And then I heard Brett whisper, "There they are."

Black silhouettes of crescent-shaped horns loomed over us against a backlit white tapestry of fog.

From Brett's larynx vibrated the words, "Seek and ye shall find."